Dear Jeanette,

Your mothers service was a very nice one & sorry I could not stay afterwards.

I hope the poems in this little book will bring you some comfort. There is a far better life than here on earth.

With Deepest Sympathy and may God Bless You.

Sharon

LIFE IS FOREVER.

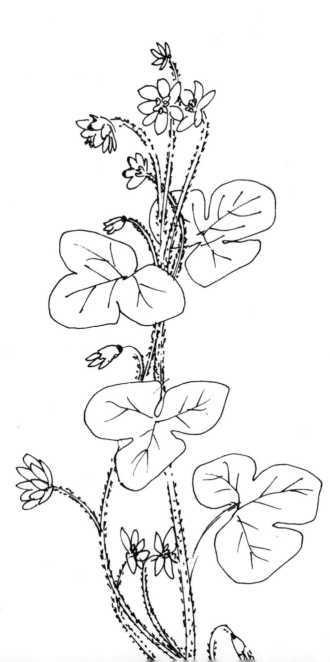

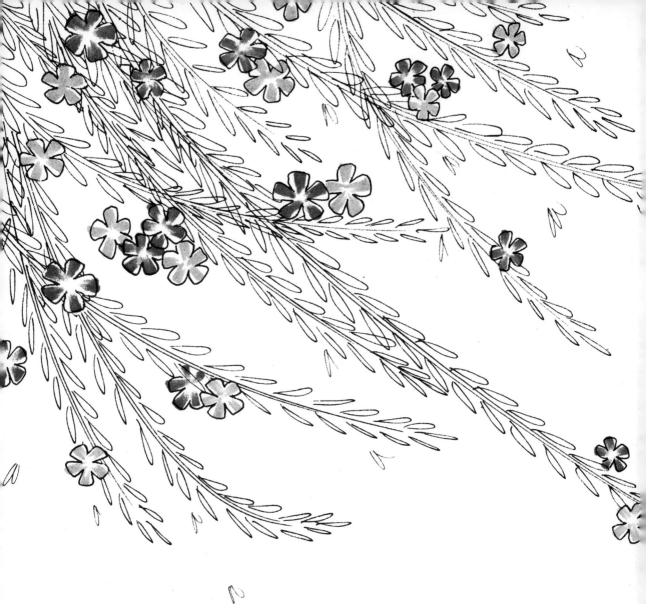

By Helen Steiner Rice

LIFE IS FOREVER

Helen Steiner Rice

GOD is LIFE
　　　　and DEATH is the WAY
Man reaches the land
　　　　of ETERNAL DAY!

Fleming H. Revell Company
Old Tappan, New Jersey

Library of Congress Cataloging in Publication Data

Rice, Helen Steiner.
  Life Is Forever.

  Poems.
  1.   Death — Poetry.   2.   Christian poetry,
American.   I.   Title.
PS3568.I28L5   811'.5'4   74-15803
ISBN 0-8007-0681-1

A Personal Letter
From the Author

Dear FRIEND,

Perhaps I am more or less of a stranger to you. But, in sorrow and tragedy, THERE ARE NO STRANGERS, and so I am reaching out my hand to you in deep and understanding sympathy.

I know the "heart-hurt" and "lost-loneliness" you are experiencing. But, after the first, stabbing anguish of grief has been softened by time, you will find great comfort in knowing that "our loved ones" are safe and free from all tears, trials, troubles, and temptations, for now they are WHERE NOTHING CAN EVER HURT THEM AGAIN!

Parting from our loved ones is something that we cannot escape, and death is just as it should be...WE ARE, and then WE ARE NOT. It is like the blowing out of a candle or the closing of a door. We go to sleep so that we may awaken in the morning, and if we did not sleep, we could never know the joy of awakening. And if we did not die, we could never LIVE ETERNALLY.

Always remember, our loved ones just go beyond the sight of our vision and the touch of our hands, and they are waiting for us "ON THE OTHER SIDE OF DEATH"...WHERE TIME IS NOT COUNTED BY YEARS and THERE ARE NO SEPARATIONS!

I have always felt, at times like this, there is so little anyone can say, for there are no words that have ever been invented to fit the loss of a loved one. But in death we find that we are drawn closer to one another and to GOD, and HEAVEN seems a little NEARER, GOD'S PROMISE a little CLEARER, and HIS LOVE a little DEARER.

We give our loved ones back to GOD. And just as HE first GAVE them to us and did not lose them in the GIVING, so we have not lost them in RETURNING them to HIM...for LIFE is ETERNAL, LOVE is IMMORTAL, DEATH is only a HORIZON, and a HORIZON is nothing but THE LIMIT OF OUR EARTHLY SIGHT.

In the poems of this book, I am trying to say that, in THE KINGDOM of THE LORD, THERE IS NOTHING LOST FOREVER...for, if we believe GOD'S PROMISE and doubt HIS GOODNESS never, we will meet all those who left us...to be TOGETHER in THE KINGDOM of FOREVER!

"LOVINGLY and PRAYERFULLY,"

Contents

LIFE IS FOREVER

Helen Steiner Rice

Nothing on Earth Is Forever Yours —
Only the Love of the Lord Endures!

Everything in life is passing
     and whatever we possess
Cannot endure forever
     but ends in nothingness,
For there are no safety boxes
     nor vaults that can contain
The possessions we collected
     and desire to retain...
So all that man acquires,
     be it power, fame or jewels,
Is but limited and earthly,
     only "treasure made for fools"...
For only in GOD'S KINGDOM
     can man find enduring treasure,
Priceless gifts of love and beauty —
     more than mortal man can measure,
And the "riches" he accumulates
     he can keep and part with never,
For only in GOD'S KINGDOM
     do our treasures last FOREVER...
So use the word FOREVER
     with sanctity and love,
For NOTHING IS FOREVER
     BUT THE LOVE OF GOD ABOVE!

Life Is Forever:
Death Is a Dream!

If we did not go to sleep at night
We'd never awaken to see the light,
And the joy of watching a new day break
Or meeting the dawn by some quiet lake
Would never be ours unless we slept
While God and all His angels kept
A vigil through this "little death"
That's over with the morning's breath—
And death, too, is a time of sleeping,
For those who die are in God's keeping
And there's a "sunrise" for each soul,
For LIFE not DEATH is God's promised goal—
So trust God's promise and doubt Him never
For only through death can man LIVE FOREVER!

I Do Not Go Alone

If DEATH should beckon me with outstretched hand
And whisper softly of "AN UNKNOWN LAND,"
I shall not be afraid to go,
For though the path I do not know,
I take DEATH'S HAND without a fear,
For He who safely brought me here
Will also take me safely back,
And though in many things I lack,
He will not let me go alone
Into the "VALLEY THAT'S UNKNOWN" ...
So I reach out and take DEATH'S HAND
And journey to the "PROMISED LAND!"

KINGS and KINGDOMS
       ALL PASS AWAY —
NOTHING ON EARTH ENDURES...
But THE LOVE of GOD
       WHO SENT HIS SON
IS FOREVER and EVER YOURS!

Spring Awakens
What Autumn Puts to Sleep

A garden of asters of varying hues,
Crimson-pinks and violet-blues,
Blossoming in the hazy Fall
Wrapped in Autumn's lazy pall—
But early frost stole in one night
And like a chilling, killing blight
It touched each pretty aster's head
And now the garden's still and dead
And all the lovely flowers that bloomed
Will soon be buried and entombed
In Winter's icy shroud of snow
But oh, how wonderful to know
That after Winter comes the Spring
To breathe new life in everything,
And all the flowers that fell in death
Will be awakened by Spring's breath—
For in God's Plan both men and flowers
Can only reach "bright, shining hours"
By dying first to rise in glory
And prove again the Easter Story.

Death Is a Doorway

On the "WINGS of DEATH"
    the "SOUL takes FLIGHT"
Into the land where
    "THERE IS NO NIGHT"—
For those who believe
    what the Saviour said
Will rise in glory
    though they be dead ...
So death comes to us
    just to "OPEN THE DOOR"
To the KINGDOM OF GOD
    and LIFE EVERMORE.

Every mile we walk in SORROW
Brings us NEARER to God's TOMORROW!

There's Always a Springtime

After the Winter comes the Spring
To show us again that in everything
There's always renewal divinely planned,
Flawlessly perfect, the work of God's Hand ...
And just like the seasons that come and go
When the flowers of Spring lay buried in snow,
God sends to the heart in its winter of sadness
A springtime awakening of new hope and gladness,
And loved ones who sleep in a season of death
Will, too, be awakened by God's life-giving breath.

All who believe
        in God's mercy and grace
Will meet their loved ones
        face to face
Where time is endless
        and joy unbroken
And only the words
        of God's love are spoken.

"Because He Lives ...
We, Too, Shall Live"

In this restless world of struggle
    it is very hard to find
Answers to the questions
    that daily come to mind—
We cannot see the future,
    what's beyond is still unknown,
For the secret of God's Kingdom
    still belongs to Him alone—
But He granted us salvation
    when His Son was crucified,
For life became immortal
    because our Saviour died.

Life is not a transient thing —
It is *CHANGE* but never *LOSS,*
For Christ purchased our salvation
When He died upon THE CROSS!

When I Must Leave You

When I must leave you
      for a little while,
Please do not grieve
      and shed wild tears
And hug your sorrow
      to you through the years,
But start out bravely
      with a gallant smile;
And for my sake
      and in my name
Live on and do
      all things the same,
Feed not your loneliness
      on empty days,
But fill each waking hour
      in useful ways,
Reach out your hand
      in comfort and in cheer
And I in turn will comfort you
      and hold you near;
And never, never
      be afraid to die,
For I am waiting
      for you in the sky!

We part with our loved ones
      but not forever
If we trust God's promise
      and doubt it never!

Each Spring,
God Renews His Promise

Long, long ago in a land far away,
There came the dawn of the first Easter Day,
And each year we see that promise reborn
That God gave the world on that first Easter Morn...
For in each waking flower and each singing bird,
The Promise of Easter is witnessed and heard,
And Spring is God's way of speaking to men
And renewing the promise of Easter again,
For death is a season that man must pass through
And, just like the flowers, God wakens him, too...
So why should we grieve when our loved ones die,
For we'll meet them again in a "cloudless sky"—
For Easter is more than a beautiful story,
It's the promise of life and Eternal Glory.

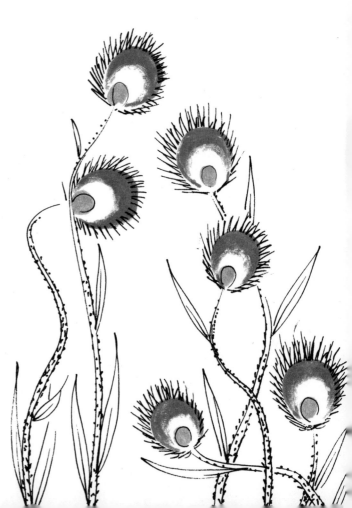

Death Is Only a Part of Life

We enter this world
     from "THE GREAT UNKNOWN"
And GOD gives each SPIRIT
     a form of its own
And endows this form
     with a heart and a soul
To spur man on
     to his ultimate goal...
For all men are born
     to RETURN as they CAME
And birth and death
     are in essence the same
And man is but born
     to die and arise
For beyond this world
     in beauty there lies
The purpose of death
     which is but to gain
LIFE EVERLASTING
     in GOD'S GREAT DOMAIN...
And no one need make
     this journey alone
For GOD has promised
     to take care of HIS own.

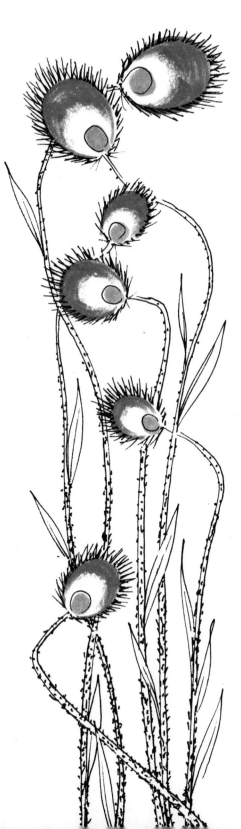

Death "bursts our chrysalis of clay"
     so that our soul is free
To soar toward ETERNITY
     to dwell in PEACE with THEE!

On the Other Side of Death

Death is a GATEWAY
        we all must pass through
To reach that Fair Land
        where the soul's born anew,
For man's born to die
        and his sojourn on earth
Is a short span of years
        beginning with birth...
And like pilgrims we wander
        until death takes our hand
And we start on our journey
        to God's Promised Land,
A place where we'll find
        no suffering nor tears,
Where TIME is not counted
        by days, months or years...
And in this Fair City
        that God has prepared
Are unending joys
        to be happily shared
With all of our loved ones
        who patiently wait
On Death's Other Side
        to open "THE GATE"!

LIVE for "ME"
And DIE for "ME"
And I, THY GOD,
Will set you FREE!

Death Opens the Door
to Life Evermore

We live a short while on earth below,
Reluctant to die for we do not know
Just what "dark death" is all about
And so we view it with fear and doubt
Not certain of what is around the bend
We look on death as the final end
To all that made us a mortal being
And yet there lies just beyond our seeing
A beautiful life so full and complete
That we should leave with hurrying feet
To walk with God by sacred streams
Amid beauty and peace beyond our dreams—
For all who believe in the RISEN LORD
Have been assured of this reward
And death for them is just "graduation"
To a higher realm of wide elevation—
For life on earth is a transient affair,
Just a few brief years in which to prepare
For a life that is free from pain and tears
Where time is not counted by hours or years—
For death is only the method God chose
To colonize heaven with the souls of those
Who by their apprenticeship on earth
Proved worthy to dwell in the land of new birth—
So death is not sad ... it's a time for elation,
A joyous transition ... the soul's emigration
Into a place where the soul's SAFE and FREE
To live with God through ETERNITY!

When DEATH STEPS IN,
        NEW LIFE BEGINS
And we rise above
        our temptations and sins!

Life Is Eternal

"LIFE IS ETERNAL," the GOOD LORD said,
So do not think of your loved one as dead —
For death is only a stepping stone
To a beautiful life we have never known,
A place where GOD promised man he would be
Eternally happy and safe and free,
A wonderful land where we live anew
When our journey on earth is over and through—
So trust in GOD and doubt HIM never
For all who love HIM live forever,
And while we cannot understand
Just let the SAVIOUR take your hand,
For when DEATH'S ANGEL comes to call
"GOD is so GREAT and we're so small"...
And there is nothing you need fear
For FAITH IN GOD makes all things clear.

"In Him We Live and Move and Have Our Being"

We walk in a world that is strange and unknown
And in the midst of the crowd we still feel alone,
We question our purpose, our part and our place
In this vast land of mystery suspended in space,
We probe and explore and try hard to explain
The tumult of thoughts that our minds entertain...
But all of our probings and complex explanations
Of man's inner feelings and fears and frustrations
Still leave us engulfed in the "MYSTERY of LIFE"
With all of its struggles and suffering and strife,
Unable to fathom what tomorrow will bring —
But there is one truth to which we can cling,
For while LIFE'S a MYSTERY man can't understand
The "GREAT GIVER of LIFE" is holding our hand
And safe in HIS care there is no need for seeing
For "IN HIM WE LIVE and MOVE and HAVE OUR BEING."

In God's Tomorrow
There Is Eternal Spring

All nature heeds the call of Spring
As GOD awakens everything,
And all that seemed so dead and still
Experiences a sudden thrill
As Springtime lays a magic hand
Across GOD'S vast and fertile land —
Oh, how can anyone stand by
And watch a sapphire Springtime sky
Or see a fragile flower break through
What just a day ago or two
Seemed barren ground still hard with frost,
But in GOD'S world no life is lost,
And flowers sleep beneath the ground
But when they hear Spring's waking sound
They push themselves through layers of clay
To reach the sunlight of GOD'S DAY —
And man, like flowers, too, must sleep
Until he is called from the "darkened deep"
To live in that place where angels sing
And where there is ETERNAL SPRING!

God Needed an Angel in Heaven

When JESUS lived upon the earth
    so many years ago,
HE called the children close to HIM
    because HE loved them so...
And with that tenderness of old,
    that same sweet, gentle way,
HE holds your little loved one close
    within HIS ARMS today...
And you'll find comfort in your faith
    that in HIS HOME ABOVE
The GOD of little children
    gives your little one HIS LOVE...
So think of your little darling
    lighthearted and happy and free
Playing in GOD'S PROMISED LAND
    where there is JOY ETERNALLY.

The Tiny "Rosebud"
God Picked to Bloom in Heaven

THE MASTER GARDENER
From HEAVEN ABOVE
Planted a seed
In THE GARDEN of LOVE
And from it there grew
A rosebud small
That never had time
To open at all,
For GOD in HIS perfect
And all-wise way
Chose this rose
For HIS HEAVENLY BOUQUET
And great was the joy
Of this tiny rose
To be the one our FATHER chose
To leave earth's garden
For ONE on high
Where roses bloom always
And never die ...
So, while you can't see
Your precious rose bloom,
You know THE GREAT GARDENER
From the "UPPER ROOM"
Is watching and tending
This wee rose with care,
Tenderly touching
Each petal so fair ...
So think of your darling
With the angels above
Secure and contented
And surrounded by love,
And remember GOD blessed
And enriched your lives, too,
For in dying your darling
Brought HEAVEN CLOSER TO YOU!

Mothers Never Die —
They Just Keep House up in the Sky

When we are children, we are happy and gay
And our MOTHER is young and she laughs as we play,
Then as we grow up, she teaches us truth
And lays life's foundation in the days of our youth —
And then it is time for us to leave home
But her teachings go with us wherever we roam,
For all that she taught us and all that we did
When we were so often just a "bad, little kid"
We will often remember and then realize
That MOTHERS ARE SPECIAL and WONDERFULLY WISE ...
And as she grows older, we look back with love
Knowing that MOTHERS ARE "GIFTS FROM ABOVE,"
And when she "goes home" to receive her reward
She will dwell in GOD'S KINGDOM and "KEEP HOUSE for THE LORD"
Where she'll "light up" the stars that shine through the night
And keep all the moonbeams "sparkling and bright"
And then with the dawn she'll put the darkness away
As she "scours" the sun to new brilliance each day ...
So dry tears of sorrow, for MOTHERS DON'T DIE —
They just move in with GOD and "KEEP HOUSE IN THE SKY,"
And there in GOD'S KINGDOM, MOTHERS watch from above
To welcome their children with their UNDYING LOVE!

"Why Should He Die for Such as I?"

In everything both great and small
We see the HAND of GOD in all,
And in the MIRACLES of Spring
When EVERYWHERE in EVERYTHING
HIS HANDIWORK is all around
And every lovely sight and sound
Proclaims the GOD of earth and sky
I ask myself JUST WHO AM I
That GOD should send HIS ONLY SON
That my salvation would be won
Upon a CROSS by a SINLESS MAN
To bring fulfillment to GOD'S PLAN —
For JESUS suffered, bled and died
That sinners might be sanctified,
And to grant GOD'S children such as I
ETERNAL LIFE in that HOME ON HIGH.

All Nature Proclaims Eternal Life

Flowers sleeping 'neath the snow,
Awakening when the Spring winds blow;
Leafless trees so bare before,
Gowned in lacy green once more;
Hard, unyielding, frozen sod
Now softly carpeted by GOD;
Still streams melting in the Spring,
Rippling over rocks that sing;
Barren, windswept, lonely hills
Turning gold with daffodils...
These MIRACLES are all around
Within our sight and touch and sound,
As true and wonderful today
As when "the stone was rolled away"
Proclaiming to all doubting men
That in GOD all things live again.

"I Know That
My Redeemer Liveth"

They asked me how I know it's true
That the Saviour lived and died ...
And if I believe the story
That the Lord was crucified?
And I have so many answers
To prove His Holy Being,
Answers that are everywhere
Within the realm of seeing ...
The leaves that fell at Autumn
And were buried in the sod
Now budding on the tree boughs
To lift their arms to God ...
The flowers that were covered
And entombed beneath the snow
Pushing through the "darkness"
To bid the Spring "hello" ...
On every side Great Nature
Retells the Easter Story—
So who am I to question
"The Resurrection Glory."

HEAVEN is REAL —
    IT'S a "POSITIVE PLACE"
Where those who believe
    MEET GOD FACE TO FACE!

"I Am the Way, the Truth, and the Life"

I AM THE WAY
      so just follow ME
Though the way be rough
      and you cannot see ...

I AM THE TRUTH
      which all men seek
So heed not "false prophets"
      nor the words that they speak ...

I AM THE LIFE
      and I hold the key
That opens the door
      to ETERNITY ...

And in this dark world
      I AM THE LIGHT
To THE PROMISED LAND
      WHERE THERE IS NO NIGHT!

The Legend of the Raindrop

The legend of the raindrop
      has a lesson for us all
As it trembled in the heavens
      questioning whether it should fall—
For the glistening raindrop argued
      to the genie of the sky,
"I am beautiful and lovely
      as I sparkle here on high,
And hanging here I will become
      part of the rainbow's hue
And I'll shimmer like a diamond
      for all the world to view" ...
But the genie told the raindrop,
      "Do not hesitate to go,
For you will be more beautiful
      if you fall to earth below,
For you will sink into the soil
      and be lost a while from sight,
But when you reappear on earth,
      you'll be looked on with delight;
For you will be the raindrop
      that quenched the thirsty ground
And helped the lovely flowers
      to blossom all around
And in your resurrection
      you'll appear in queenly clothes
With the beauty of the lily
      and the fragrance of the rose;
Then, when you wilt and wither,
      you'll become part of the earth
And make the soil more fertile
      and give new flowers birth" ...
For there is nothing ever lost
      or ETERNALLY NEGLECTED,
For EVERYTHING GOD EVER MADE
      IS ALWAYS RESURRECTED;
So trust God's all-wise wisdom
      and doubt the Father never,
For in HIS HEAVENLY KINGDOM
      THERE IS NOTHING LOST FOREVER.

As Long As You Live and Remember —
Your Loved One Lives in Your Heart!

May tender memories
      soften your grief,
May fond recollection
      bring you relief,
And may you find comfort
      and peace in the thought
Of the joy that knowing
      your loved one brought —
For time and space
      can never divide
Or keep your loved one
      from your side
When memory paints
      in colors true
The happy hours
      that belonged to you.

A Consolation Meditation

On the wings
　　　　of death and sorrow
God sends us
　　　　new hope for tomorrow —
And in His mercy
　　　　and His grace
He gives us strength
　　　　to bravely face
The lonely days
　　　　that stretch ahead
And know our loved one
　　　　is not dead
But only sleeping
　　　　and out of our sight
And we'll meet in that land
　　　　WHERE THERE IS NO NIGHT.

In the Hands of God Even Death Is a Time for Rejoicing

And so when death brings weeping
　　　　and the heart is filled with sorrow,
It beckons us to seek GOD
　　　　as we ask about "TOMORROW" ...
And in these hours of "heart-hurt"
　　　　we draw closer to believing
That even death in GOD'S HANDS
　　　　is not a cause for grieving
But a time for joy in knowing
　　　　death is just a stepping-stone
To a LIFE that's EVERLASTING
　　　　such as we have never known.